Dreams

By the Same Author

Drums, Rattles, and Bells
Flutes, Whistles, and Reeds
Gliders
Horns
Kites
Magic Made Easy
The Magic of Sound
Puzzle Patterns
Shadows
Singing Strings
Song, Speech, and Ventriloquism
Spinning Tops
Spooky Magic

Dreams

written and illustrated by
LARRY KETTELKAMP

William Morrow & Company *New York*

Published simultaneously in Canada by George J. McLeod Limited, Toronto

Printed in the United States of America.

Library of Congress Catalog Card Number 68-14803

Thanks is given by the author to Dr. Stanley Krippner, Director, Dream Laboratory, Community Mental Health Center, Maimonides Medical Center, Brooklyn, New York, for his helpful suggestions.

Picture credits:
54 and 55, Drawn from tracings supplied by the Downstate Medical Center, Brooklyn, New York.
64 and 65, *The New York Times*
82, Dr. Stanley Krippner.
84, Collection Whitney Museum of American Art, New York.

Numbers of the day are fragmentary
Symbols of the act of cash and carry,
Never done.

Night's abacus frames the trinity
Of me, myself, and yet to be
But not begun.

Hold, wish, win the rhythm of the heart;
Dream, the dreamer, and his art—
These three are one.

Contents

Introduction

Did you dream last night? Everyone does several times each night. Whether you remember or not, you are a regular dream maker. This discovery is one that has been made about dreams and their importance within the last few years. Sleep laboratories are hard at work investigating the process of dreaming and supplying fascinating new information about this familiar experience.

People have always been curious about dreams. As far back as written records can be found there are accounts of dreams and attempts to understand them. Some thought they were the work of a god or a devil. Some thought they foretold future events.

Were dreams a bad or a good influence? The only certain thing was that the dream was mysterious. To the dreamer the events of a dream seemed real. Only when he awoke did he know he had been dreaming. And things happened in dreams that could not possibly happen during waking hours. Something appeared to be let out of a hidden part of the mind at night in a way that the dreamer could not control.

Scientists in the nineteenth century took

a new interest in dreams as a key to the secrets of the subconscious mind. Today sleep and dreams are being investigated through the use of new electronic equipment, and once again people are speculating about whether dreams can foretell the future.

Why is the mind so active when the body is sleeping? How do we know that everyone dreams? How long do dreams last? Some of these questions are just now being answered. And some of the answers have upset common beliefs. But the age-old ideas about dreams are still important. Truth is sometimes known before it is fully understood.

Ancient
Beliefs

THE EGYPTIANS

As long as there have been records, in
pictures or in writing, people have kept
accounts of their dreams and of the supposed meaning of them. The oldest known
dream book comes from Egypt. It has been
dated about 1350 B.C., making it more

than 3,000 years old. This Chester Beatty papyrus is named after the man who donated it to the British Museum. Ideas found in it are still being used by some people today in dream interpretation.

The book contains about 200 dreams and an interpretation of each one. The dreams are divided into favorable and unfavorable ones. The dream of sawing wood is good because it means that your enemies will perish. However, the dream of teeth falling out means that members of your own family will bring death to you. Many of these dream interpretations have a meaning just the opposite of what happens in the dream. To dream of death, for instance, signifies that you will have a long life.

The ancient Egyptians tried to make use of dreams by a practice called incubation. A sick or troubled person took a special medicine that stimulated dreaming, and then spent the night sleeping in a temple. During the night he was supposed to have a dream that would help him to overcome his problem through the assistance of the god in whose temple he had slept.

DREAMS IN THE BIBLE

The Old Testament of the Bible has many records of dreams. Perhaps the most famous is Jacob's dream of the ladder reaching up to heaven, reported in the twenty-eighth chapter of Genesis. The account begins, "And he dreamed, and behold a ladder set up on the earth, and the top of it reached to heaven: and behold the angels of God ascending and descending on it."

Throughout the Bible dreams are re-

ported as messages from God. A state-
ment in the book of Numbers reads,
"Hear now my words: If there be a
prophet among you, I the Lord will
make myself known unto him in a
vision, and will speak to him in a
dream."

Many of these dreams needed special interpretation in order to be understood. A good example is Pharaoh's dream of seven fat cows that were devoured by seven lean ones, and seven good ears of corn that were devoured by seven poor ears. Pharaoh tried in vain to understand his dream until finally Joseph was able to interpret it for him. The seven fat cows and the good ears of corn stood for seven rich years of harvest. The seven lean cows and seven poor ears of corn stood for seven years of poor crops that would follow. During this second period all of the stores of food would be used up, and there would be a famine throughout the country.

The Jews of the Old Testament as well as the early Egyptians believed that dreams used symbols, which had to be interpreted. That is, the objects in the dream usually stood for something else.

THE GREEKS AND ROMANS

The Greek civilization that flourished several hundred years before the Christian era held dreams to be of great importance. The Greeks practiced incubation in much the same way as the ancient Egyptians, except, of course, they substituted their own gods in place of those of the Egyptians.

The Greek philosopher Aristotle had much to say about dreams. He tried to overcome superstitious ideas and explain dreams in a reasonable way. He thought that some dreams were bound to come true simply because so many people had so many different dreams. He pointed out that nighttime dreams often influenced the mood of a person during the following day, and he realized that a dream could reveal to a person symptoms

of an illness he was developing before they were noticed by the waking mind.

Two centuries later a Roman named Artemidorus gave his whole attention to recording and interpreting dreams. His ideas were to shape the course of dream study for hundreds of years. Artemidorus wrote a book called *Oneirocritica,* which can be translated, the interpretation of dreams. This book became so popular that translations of it were still being published sixteen centuries after it was written.

Artemidorus took a flexible approach to the understanding of dreams. He realized that not only were there good dreams and bad, but that a single dream might be partly good and partly bad. He also felt that the interpretation must depend upon the dreamer. Meanings could be different for different people. Here, from his book, is Artemidorus's interpretation of a dream about a rainbow.

To dream you see a rainbow denotes the changing of your present estate and manner of life. To dream of seeing a rainbow in the East is a good omen to the poor and sick; for the former will recover their estates, and the latter their health. To dream of seeing a rainbow in the West, to the rich is a good, to the poor, a bad sign. Note, also, that in your dreams the rainbow on the right hand is good, and on the left, ill; and you must judge the right or the left according to the sun. And in what quality soever it appears, it is a good sign to anyone that is afflicted with poverty or any other affliction, for it changeth the time and the air.

Artemidorus's interpretations have been carried over into many popular dream books, but his work also was useful to those who began the serious study of dreams hundreds of years after he had lived.

The Study
of Dreams

A NEW SCIENCE

Toward the end of the nineteenth century a group of German thinkers, interested in the study of the mind, turned
their attention to that part of the mind
that is active during sleep. They called it
the unconscious—to distinguish it from

the ordinary consciousness. Sometimes it is also called the subconscious. These investigators became known as psychologists, from the Greek word that means mind, or personality.

FREUD

About this time a young Viennese medical student named Sigmund Freud became interested in treating mental illness. Patients often told him of their dreams, and the dreams seemed to Freud to offer an insight into their problems. In order to understand their dreams Freud developed a technique called association. He let the patient talk freely about an idea or object in his dream. It would remind the patient of another object. Soon a chain of related objects or ideas was begun. In this way hidden ideas could be found behind the story of the dream. The discovery of these hidden thoughts could often help the patient to understand his illness and actually make some improvement. In this way the patient was helped to know his real self.

Freud developed a regular method of using dreams to help people overcome problems. He called his method psychoanalysis, which meant analyzing the mind or personality. In 1900 Freud wrote a book that was to begin the modern study of dreams. He gave his book the same title as that used by the Roman, Artemidorus, centuries earlier. It was called *The Interpretation of Dreams.*

Freud's work was not easy for him to accomplish. He was trying to set up a scientific study of the human personality by means of dreams. At first his book and his ideas were laughed at. He was handicapped by the lack of reliable records of people's dreams. Freud had to begin with those of his own patients, and in order not to embarrass them he used his own dreams as examples in his book.

Freud believed that personality troubles came from the basic desires we all have.

Sigmund Freud

These desires are very strong in childhood, but since we cannot often do as we please we are forced to hold them back. Those desires that could not be expressed became buried and forgotten by the everyday conscious mind. This forgetting is called repression, which means to press back again. But these memories of childhood desires always remained in the subconscious mind. In dreams all through life they expressed themselves as wishes. But since the wish itself might shock us, it was always disguised by the symbols and the story of the dream. This way the wishes could be fulfilled without shocking or hurting anyone. Freud saw the dream as a safety valve. He called the dream "the guardian of sleep."

In time the importance of Freud's work was recognized. Not everyone agreed with his conclusions about the meaning of dreams. But his methods and discoveries have become a fundamental part of the study of personality.

OTHER THEORIES

A younger friend of Freud's also became very interested in the meaning of dreams. His name was Carl Jung, and he, too, had started out by studying medicine. Because of his interest in his own subconscious mind, Jung turned to psychology and the treatment of his patients through their dreams.

Jung did not agree that all dreams were due to repressed childhood desires. He believed that dreams came from many sources. Some dreams were great insights from beyond the ordinary experience of the dreamer. Some contained ideas that the dreamer could not possibly have

Carl Jung

learned about during his own lifetime. Jung suggested that men could inherit certain dream symbols from generation to generation. He spoke of a "collective unconscious." This part of the mind, he believed, was common to all people everywhere and accounted for the great similarity of dreams among people who had lived in different times and places.

Jung spent much time studying mythology. He thought that the themes of legends and fairy tales were the same as some of those found in dreams. These similar characters or ideas Jung named archetypes. Two are the Wise Old Man and the Earth Mother. Jung said that when a wise old man appeared in a legend or a dream, he stood for the idea of all that was spiritual or creative. The earth mother represented that which was practical and down-to-earth.

Freud had said that we all had similar basic desires. They were crude but formed the basis of dream wishes. Jung said that we share common noble ideas as well, and that dreams represented the best in us as well as the worst.

To the ideas of Freud and Jung, modern psychologists have added their own interpretations. Now there are records of

thousands of individual dreams available for study. Many men have spent the larger part of their working lives using dreams as an important means of helping people solve their problems.

Today dreams are thought to be work that we do in an effort to balance our personalities and to grow and mature. Dreams will not let us forget those situations we would rather avoid. Instead, we are forced to face each problem and try to solve it. Sometimes a dream is action that we portray as it might actually happen if we had more courage than we do. In this way the dream can be a safety valve to let off emotional energy. Or the dream may suggest a good solution to a troubling situation. We may be able to use the plan of the dream in waking life and find that it is successful.

A person who is quiet and shy during

the day may have wild and fantastic dreams. Or a person who seems very aggressive may find that in his dreams he has become fearful and hesitant. The dream apparently warns us, "Look, you may think you know the kind of person you are, but you are mistaken. Here is how things really are."

A healthy person works toward the blending of his outer self and his inner self. And dreams can be an important means of discovering the inner self.

DREAM SYMBOLS

Modern psychoanalysts agree that many dream objects stand for something else in a symbolic way. And they believe that the exact meaning of the symbol depends on the dreamer and his personality. However, some symbols have been found to mean

much the same thing for many people. Here are some that are common.

Kings and queens may represent the parents of the dreamer. Other exalted figures may have the same meaning. Small animals may stand for children. Crossing a river can mean meeting an important turning point in life. Failure to get to the other side may mean failure to meet this challenge. Getting across can mean success in making a fresh start.

A long journey may sometimes be associated with death and the idea of
going on to another place or exist-
ence. Catching a train or plane may
mean concern with the possibility of
death. Missing the ride could suggest
that death is postponed.

A bridge may represent a way of overcoming an obstacle. Crossing the
bridge may mean success in solving

the problem. Since a bridge is a direct way of crossing a river, it may represent a smooth path to a fresh start if it is crossed.

A road or path often represents the journey of life. Turnoffs and intersections may stand for choices that have to be made in life.

A house often stands for the body or the mind of the dreamer. Rooms of the house may represent parts of the

body. The upper and lower stories of a house may represent the conscious and subconscious levels of the mind. The basement may suggest hidden fears, wishes, or knowledge.

A crab may be a response to a physical sensation. The pincers of a crab are sometimes associated with the feeling of a stomach ache. Something that upsets the body in this region may trigger a nightmare of a crablike creature.

All of these objects or ideas appear again and again in dreams. Whenever the common meanings make sense, such objects can be called universal symbols.

CREATIVE DREAMS

The work of poets, artists, musicians, research scientists, and others who create

Wolfgang Amadeus
Mozart

new things and develop fresh ideas is sometimes carried forward in dreams, which are called creative.

There are many examples of creative dreams. The composer Mozart spoke of finished musical pieces that occurred to him as dreams. Here is a part of a letter he wrote describing how this happened.

The whole, though it be long, stands almost complete and finished in my mind, so that I can survey it, like a fine picture or a beautiful statue, at a glance. Nor do I hear in my imagination the parts successively, but I hear them, as it were, all at once. What a delight this is I cannot tell! All this inventing, this producing, takes place in a lively dream. . . . What has been thus produced I do not easily forget, and this is perhaps the best gift I have my Divine Maker to thank for. "

The poet Samuel Taylor Coleridge recorded a similar experience before writing the poem, "Kubla Khan." Coleridge was not feeling well and had taken a prescription. He soon fell asleep in his chair just as he was reading these words from a book: "Here the Khan Kubla commanded a palace to be built, and a stately garden thereunto. And thus ten miles of fertile ground were enclosed with a wall." Coleridge slept for about three hours. During that time he dreamed that images rose up before him, and that these images suggested words to express themselves. He felt that perhaps two or three hundred lines were composed for him by his inner mind. When he awoke, he began quickly to write down the lines. After putting down the first ten lines he was interrupted by a visitor. Following the visit, Coleridge could no longer remember the rest of the exact lines he had dreamed. But he was able to use the memory of the dream to construct a finished poem.

The author and poet, Robert Louis Stevenson, used the contents of his dreams for his work. Stevenson writes that when he was very young he often had nightmares, a phase that many children go through and soon outgrow. Later he had dreams about enjoyable travels. Finally, he began to dream whole stories. What was more, a story might be continued in a series of several dreams from night to night.

At times Stevenson felt that he led a double life, that of his dreams and that of his waking experiences. In fact, he wrote a story about his fears of this double life. It was the famous story of the man who sometimes became a monster, "Dr. Jekyll and Mr. Hyde." In spite of his fears, Stevenson was able to use his dreams to help him produce stories throughout his life.

One of the best-known creative dreams is that of a German chemist named August Kekulé. For a long time Kekulé had been trying to figure out how the molecules fit together in a chemical called trimethyl benzene. There seemed to be no answer. Finally one night he had a dream, which he later reported.

"The atoms were juggling before my eyes . . . my mind's eye, sharpened by repeated sights of a similar kind, could now distinguish larger structures of different forms and in long chains, many of them close together; everything was moving in a snakelike and twisting manner. Suddenly, what was this? One of the snakes got hold of its own tail and the whole structure was mockingly twisting in front of my eyes." At this point Kekulé awoke with a start. He now knew that the molecules of benzene were arranged in a ring!

Why doesn't everyone have creative dreams? To be sure, these men whose dreams have been described were all talented. But more than that, they worked

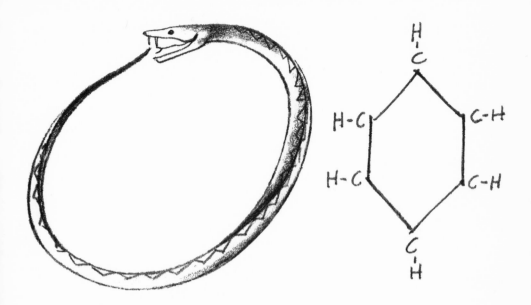

Kekulé's dream and his discovery

very hard and spent much time trying
again and again to achieve what they
were after. In addition, these men all had
a high respect for their inner minds. They
realized that the subconscious could or-
ganize memories that the conscious mind
had neglected. They were alert to any information from the subconscious, whether

it was expected or not. And some of this work was done in dreams as they slept.

To trust the subconscious is to have faith in a part of yourself that you cannot directly control. It requires patience. And it takes willingness to accept that which seems new or different. But the subconscious needs its counterpart, the conscious, and the wakeful conscious cannot grow without the work of the subconscious. When the two minds work together, amazing results are possible.

Sleep Research

THE CONSCIOUS MIND

When we are awake, our bodies respond to conditions and happenings in the outside world. We focus our attention on our actions. We concentrate usually on one thing at a time. If there are interruptions, then we must pay attention to them. We must worry about feeding our bodies and protecting them from harsh weather or injury. We think of causes and results. Our thoughts must fit the rules of the outside world.

The state in which wakeful activity takes place is commonly called consciousness. The special qualities of wakeful consciousness are focus and will. Of our own free will we can direct or focus attention on just one part of the outside world at a time. We control our actions. And we use from our memories only that which helps our actions. Other memories are forgotten. We can say that we live within the limits of physical time and space. We live in the solid world of three dimensions—depth, width, and height— plus a fourth dimension—which we experience as the smooth flow of time. This world is the one that we are conscious of.

THE SUBCONSCIOUS

During sleep another type of mind takes over, the subconscious, which has been kept in the background behind the conscious mind during the day. But now, during sleep, it is free to work. The subconscious is a sort of opposite or counterpart to the conscious mind.

Actually, psychologists have identified many different levels, or kinds, of consciousness. Wakeful or controlled consciousness may include shades of alertness or dullness and such states as the daydream or the trance. States with a lack of wakeful awareness include the various stages of sleep. Sometimes consciousness seems to be expanded or to be a combination of several states at the same time.

But the states of the mind seem always to fall into one of the two general categories, that which is concerned with the outside world, or that which relates to the inner world. Whether the inner mind is called the unconscious or the subconscious, its activities are no less important than those of the wakeful conscious. Many times they are more important.

The subconscious is not confined by the outside world and the ordinary limits of time and space. During sleep memories that were not useful during the day may be recalled. The memories may be very old or very recent. The subconscious is a storehouse of memories of everything one has ever experienced. Ideas and memories can be brought together in a way that makes sense to the inner self, but which might not follow the rules of the outside world. The new ideas may have some connection with the events of the daytime world. Events may seem to happen as they would in waking life, but with strange differences.

When asleep, the drowsy conscious mind seems to be a quiet spectator in a theater. The subconscious writes the play, chooses the actors, and sets the stage. The result is seen by the conscious mind as a dream.

DREAM LABORATORIES

Within the last twenty-five years studies have revealed that sleep, a state in which we spend one third of our lives, is not simply resting the body and mind from daytime activity. There is a pattern to a full night of sleep, and it is much the same for all of us. The dream is a part of the natural rhythm of sleep.

Pioneering sleep research has been done at the University of Chicago by Nathaniel Kleitman, who developed laboratory tests in this field. A first clue about the natural rhythm of sleep came from a student of Kleitman's named Eugene Aserinsky. Aserinsky was studying the sleep of newborn babies. He noticed that from time to time as the babies slept, their eyes seemed to move beneath the closed eyelids. All of the babies showed this behavior, and there seemed to be a pattern of eyes moving then stopping and then moving again. Similar activity seemed to occur among adults, while they slept. Were eye movements common to everyone during sleep? And did eye movements occur during dreams? Some more exact way of studying this phenomenon was needed.

Sometime earlier a useful discovery had been made by Hans Berger at the University of Jena in Germany. To study brain activity he attached wires to metal discs called electrodes. These devices were then fastened to the heads of volunteers. The wires picked up tiny changes in electric currents. They were strengthened, or amplified, a million times, and a machine converted the signals into pen and ink tracings on graph paper. Dr. Berger showed that in the brain there was constant electrical activity, and that it varied as the volunteer was calm or excited, asleep or awake. Machines of this kind came to be called electroencephalographs. *Cephalo* means *head,* and *graph* means *picture,* so the name means simply, electric-head-picture. The pen tracings are called electroencephalograms. They have been nicknamed brain waves, or E'grams, and the machine's name itself is shortened to EEG.

Kleitman and Aserinsky began using the EEG to measure eye movements as well as the brain's electrical changes. The usual electrodes were fastened to the scalp. Two more electrodes were used for the eyes, one attached at each outer corner. The muscle movements of the eyes created tiny electric charges that could be amplified and traced on graph paper, along with the activity of the brain itself. Now there was a way of determining the patterns of sleep for the first time.

THE STAGES OF SLEEP

Measurements revealed that the full night's sleep of an adult showed a pattern that repeated itself about every hour and a half. The pattern occurred about four to six times each night.

The EEG tracings suggested that there were four general stages of sleep. Just before dropping off but while still awake, the brain puts out a regular rhythmic impulse about ten times each second. It is called the alpha rhythm. The sleeper's eyelids have closed, but his eyes still move about beneath the lids.

Now comes stage one. The eyes stop their quick movements and roll lazily in their sockets or become quiet. The brain rhythm may show occasional waves of from four to six pulses each second. This is called the theta rhythm. The sleeper is in a very light sleep. Heartbeat and breathing have begun to slow down.

In stage two the tracings often show two new kinds of configuration. First, there is once in a while a slow burst of electrical activity that seems to spill over from the brain and shows on both eye and brain tracings at the same time. These bursts may also sometimes appear during other stages. Second, a rapid brain

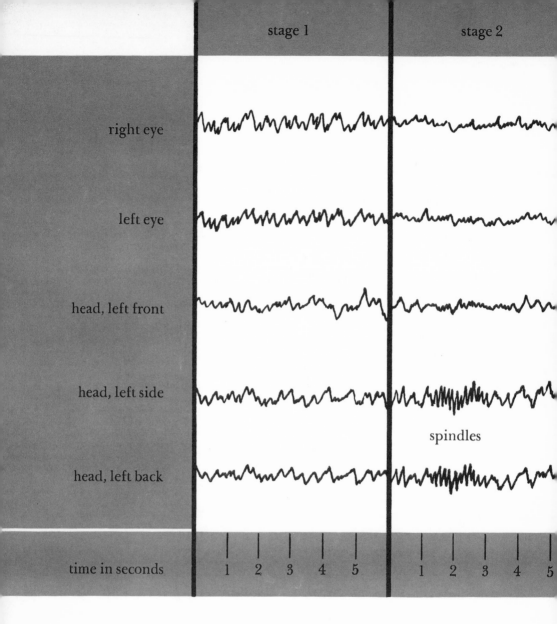

EEG TRACINGS, SAMPLES OF THE STAGES OF SLEEP

Notice the fast spindles in stage 2,
the slow delta rhythm in stage 4,
and the rapid eye movements in REM stage 1.

stage 3 stage 4 REM stage 1

rapid eye movements

delta waves

1 2 3 4 5 1 2 3 4 5 1 2 3 4 5

When eye tracings converge,
eyes are moving to the right.
When the tracings separate,
eyes are moving to the left.

EEG pattern sometimes comes about twelve to fourteen times each second, making rough and jagged tracings, called spindles. Stage two is still a light sleep, but heartbeat and breathing are usually a little slower than in stage one.

In stage three a very slow brain rhythm begins to appear. The pulses come from one to three times each second and are called delta waves. Stage four is similar to three but the delta waves become more regular. By stage four heartbeat and breathing are generally slower than at any other time. The body is quiet, but muscles still have some tone or tension. The eyes are quiet except for some echo of the slow delta rhythm.

DREAM SLEEP

Now comes the most unusual stage of

all. It is sometimes called paradoxical sleep, because it is in some ways light and in some ways deep. The eyes begin to move as they do when the person is awake, and the alpha rhythm, which was present just before falling asleep, comes back at about eight pulses each second. This sleep is considered a variation of stage one sleep. But the eyes that became quiet during the first stage one now are busy. Thus, this new kind of stage one is called REM, which stands for rapid eye movements. If awakened now, the sleeper will almost always report a dream. His heartbeat may quicken and his breathing may become more rapid. In spite of all this activity, the sleeper may claim that he was in deep sleep if he is awakened. In fact, the muscles of his head and his neck may relax completely during this stage. Such characteristics make up the paradox of REM, the sleep of the dream.

After the dreaming phase of stage one the sleeper repeats the cycle, going through stages two, three, and four again, then back to stage one with another dream. This pattern is the one that occurs about four to six times each night.

The experimenters noticed that dreams tend to last longer and longer throughout the night. The first dream might last only about ten minutes. The next might last about twenty minutes, and so on until the last dream of the night, which might take as much as forty-five minutes. Altogether about one fourth of the night was spent in dreaming.

The deepest sleep came earlier in the night. As dreams grew longer the sleeper spent less time in stages two, three, and four. Near morning he might skip stages three and four entirely. The pattern con-

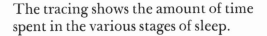

A TYPICAL SLEEP PATTERN

The tracing shows the amount of time
spent in the various stages of sleep.

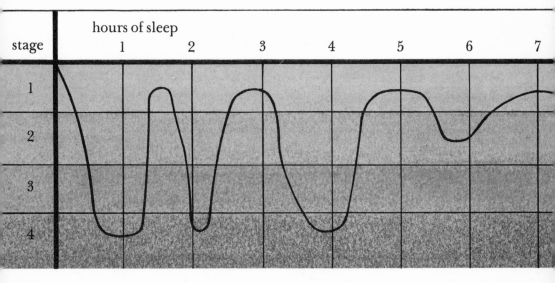

sisted mostly of a change from a long
dream to stage two, then back to stage
one and another dream.

It has been found that dreamlike experiences may also occur in stages of sleep
other than the REM stage. But in general
true dreams occur during REM periods
and the four stages of sleep tend to follow
a regular cycle.

Where did this natural dream rhythm come from? It was known that newborn babies sleep for periods of about one hour, with short periods of wakefulness in between. By the time a child is several years old, the sleep periods are a little longer, about an hour and ten minutes. Some of the periods become grouped together during the night. The child does not quite awaken between periods, so that they run together. During the day the young child still naps, a leftover from the time when day and night were broken into short sleep periods. As a child grows older, the daytime sleep periods are dropped entirely. In their place a group of periods, each about an hour and a half long, run together to make about eight hours of nighttime sleep. In this way the sleep rhythm of an adult is still much the same as the sleeping-waking pattern shown in a young baby's sleep.

Babies experience REM sleep even before they are born, and when newly born about half of their sleep time is spent in REM sleep. After the age of one year the amount of REM sleep drops to about one third of the total time spent in sleep. A young adult spends about one fourth of the night dreaming. For an elderly person the dream time amounts to only about one fifth of the total.

How important is dream sleep? In the mid 1950's two men decided to find out. They were Dr. William Dement and Dr. Charles Fisher, who were working at Mount Sinai Hospital in New York. Volunteers came to spend several nights in the laboratory. They were allowed to sleep through the night as usual, except when one thing happened. Each time the EEG machine showed the start of a dream period, the volunteer was awakened, then allowed to sleep again. These volunteers got all of their regular sleep except for their dream time. After only about five nights of dreamless sleep, the volunteers became jittery and anxious. They had trouble concentrating and one volunteer quit in a panic.

At the same time another group of volunteers were awakened the same number of times as those in the first group. The difference was that they were awakened when they were not dreaming. These volunteers were able to get about the usual amount of dream sleep. The second group of volunteers had none of the troubles and upsets of the first group. This experiment was the first evidence that regular dream sleep was necessary in order for a person to function well during the day.

Some volunteers have gone as long as

fifteen nights without dream sleep. With each successive night the volunteers tried more and more often to dream. After many nights the volunteers tried to dream all of the time and had to be awakened constantly. As soon as the awakenings were stopped, and the volunteers were allowed a regular night's sleep, they spent much more time than usual in dream sleep. This behavior continued until the loss of dream time was made up.

These recent experiments have shown that dreaming seems as necessary to us as eating and drinking. Experiments using the EEG with animals have revealed that REM sleep is characteristic of all the mammals, including human beings. Reptiles such as turtles and snakes do not dream. But the mammals all spend large amounts of time in the paradoxical sleep of dreams.

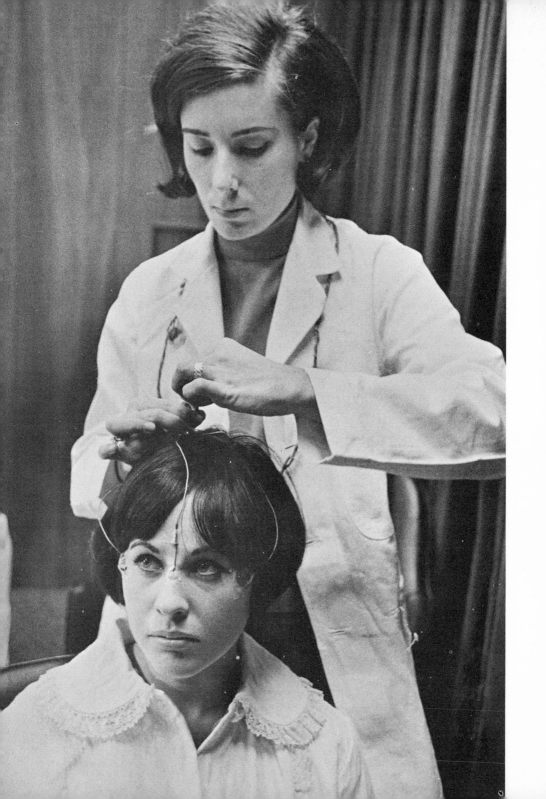

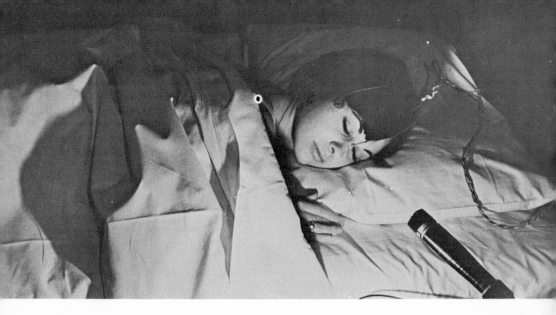

A sleep volunteer is wired for
the EEG machine. During the night
she can be awakened during REM
periods. Dream reports can be
recorded and studied later.

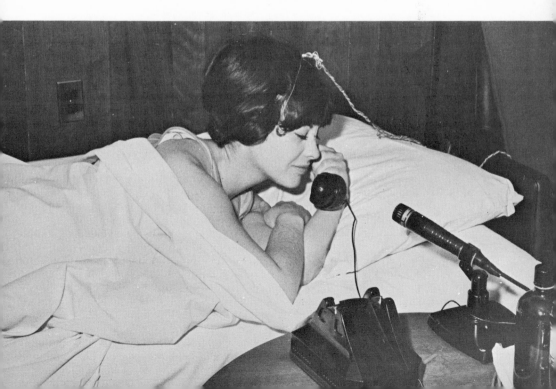

SLEEP CHEMISTRY

Is there something in the human body that automatically triggers the dream periods of sleep? Scientists have known for some time that non-dreaming sleep could be caused by electrical stimulation of various parts of the brain. They also have known that various chemicals could increase or decrease the tendency to dream.

At the Columbia University School of Medicine careful experiments have shown that very small doses of LSD 25 can cause large increases in the length of dream time in sleep. LSD and similar chemicals that stimulate dreaming are called psychedelics, which means mind-manifesting. Other drugs such as chloropromazine and reserpine may reduce the tendency to dream. These drugs are known as tranquilizers. Already both tranquilizers and psychedelics have proved useful in treating mental illness. Mental health seems to depend upon the proper balance between a dreaming mind and a wakeful mind.

Can it be that the body produces its own chemicals to regulate this balance? Experiments have shown that such chemical changes do take place, and the changes are related to certain areas of the brain.

The top portion of the brain is associated with thought. It is the cerebral cortex. At the base of the brain the spinal nervous system extends upward to tuck in between the two halves of the brain. In this region lies a network of nerve cells called the reticular formation. The name comes from the Latin word *rete,* which means *net.* Sensory impulses, such as those from the skin, eyes, and ears, pass upward through the reticular formation. Just above the reticular formation is the

Wakeful thought is stimulated by impulses
from the ARAS which join sensory signals
coming to the cortex. During sleep the
ARAS signals become weaker and sensory
signals are not translated into actions.

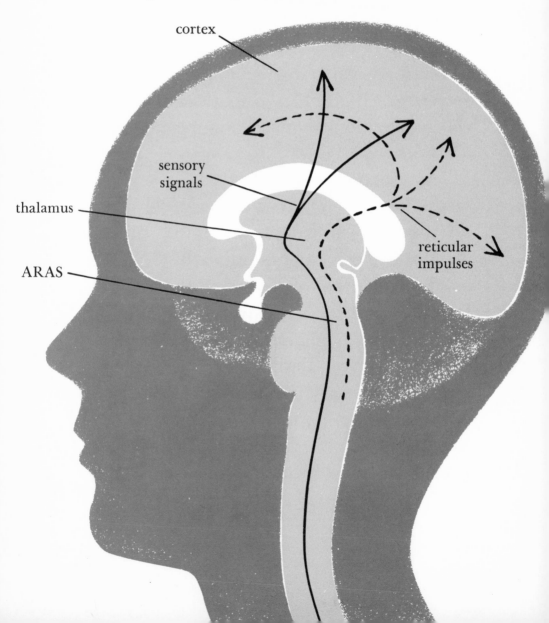

cortex

sensory
signals

thalamus

ARAS

reticular
impulses

thalamus. Some sensations stop there. Others pass through the thalamus to various parts of the cortex. There they are analyzed and translated into actions.

This pathway at the base of the brain is called the ascending reticular activating system, or ARAS, for short. When certain special impulses in ARAS are added to the sensory impulses coming through to the brain, the person is awake and able to act. When the special reticular impulses are too weak, the person is asleep. Then some of the sensory impulses that reach the cortex may be formed into part of a dream, instead of into actions.

Dr. Raul Hernandez-Peon, working in Mexico City, is one of many researchers who are using chemicals to trace the brain patterns of sleep. Such experiments can lead to a better understanding of just how we dream and sleep.

A branch of the United States Government called the National Institute of Mental Health has played an important part in making new sleep research possible. Funds have been granted to many sleep laboratories and hospitals all over the country. Today is an exciting time for discoveries about the importance of sleep and dreams in our lives.

Psychic Dreams

DREAM PREDICTIONS

Sleep and dream research has stimulated new interest in psychic dreams. Basically *psychic* means simply, of the mind or personality, but this word has come to be used for a special quality of mind. It is the quality of being beyond the normal.

Such qualities or abilities are also called paranormal, meaning again, greater than the normal.

An unusual but not rare psychic experience is the dream that seems to predict the future. Such dream predictions sometimes come true in a startling way. The modern psychologist, Erich Fromm, gives an example of a puzzling dream he had that later came true.

He was to meet an important man for the first time. Everyone had told him that this man was very kind and generous. When Fromm first spoke to the man he had a fleeting feeling that he did not quite trust him. However, they began to talk and Fromm found him to be just as everyone said, and Fromm left him feeling that this man was indeed an unusually fine person.

But that night Fromm had a dream

that the same man had done something quite dishonest. This dream surprised him, and he could not understand why he should dream such a thing. However, soon the man did indeed act dishonestly just as Fromm had dreamed. Fromm then remembered that when he had first met him, he had had a sudden feeling of mistrust. But his friends had said that he was a fine man so Fromm had ignored his feeling and come to the same conclusion as everyone else.

Fromm suggests that subconsciously he was actually aware of qualities in the man that gave him doubts. These observations were pushed aside by the conscious mind, but remained in the subconscious. Later these observations formed the basis of a logical prediction in a dream. The dream prediction was a surprise to the waking mind only because it had chosen not to believe all of the facts that could be seen.

Often someone will dream that he is ill with a certain disease. In waking life there is no trace of sickness. But weeks, months, or sometimes even years later that exact disease develops. Sometimes more than one dream warns of the coming illness. Again the subconscious simply may be aware of symptoms of sickness before they are strong enough to be noticed during waking hours. The dream is a logical prediction based on the facts at hand.

But there are many dreams of future events that cannot be explained so easily. The author Rudyard Kipling dreamed of being at a ceremony in Westminster Abbey. In the dream a man came up, put his hand on Kipling's arm, and said, "I want a word with you, please." Just over a month later the exact events he had dreamed took place down to the last detail. After attending a ceremony in Westminster Abbey, a man did come over to him, touch his arm, and say, "I want a word with you, please."

Abraham Lincoln reported a dream to his friends that has since become famous. In his dream he saw himself walking from room to room in the White House. He heard people crying, but could see no one. He walked into the East Room, where there was a coffin. There were soldiers acting as guards, and a crowd of people weeping. The President questioned one of the guards. "Who is dead in the White House?" "The President," answered the guard. "He was assassinated." Only a few days after the dream, President Lincoln was killed by the assassin, John Wilkes Booth.

Recently a woman named Jeane Dixon

has become famous in the United States for her predictions of important political events. Some of them have occurred just as she predicted. Part of this information she has translated from the stories and symbols of her dreams.

A friend of mine told of a dream that turned out to be an unusual prediction. Her family was to move to another town, and they were starting to look for a house. She had a dream that showed her family living in another home. The dream had details about the arrangements of the rooms and the style of the house. However, the house they actually bought and moved into did not seem to match that of the dream, and she forgot all about it.

Sometime later a neighbor who had known that particular house for many years was speaking to her about it. The house had been extensively remodeled.

The neighbor described the arrangement of the rooms as they used to be. Suddenly my friend realized that the old original house was exactly the one she had seen in her earlier dream! She was indeed living in the house her dream had predicted, but had not recognized it because of the remodeling.

I myself had a similar house dream before a recent move. At first I did not know what it all meant. In my dream I had walked along a highway and crossed a bridge. This action I could understand represented the change I was about to make. Crossing a bridge sometimes stands for overcoming a problem and making a fresh start. Then in my dream I saw a house that was built in a ranch style, except that at one end there was a two-story section. I seemed to be looking in at an upstairs window, wanting to enter the house. The window seemed blocked with crossbars. The house was empty, and suddenly I was standing inside.

About two months later my family and I made plans to buy a new house in another town. Suddenly I remembered the dream I could not understand. The house in my dream had the same shape as the one we moved into. In my dream the house had horizontal siding, and our actual house had shingles. However, a drawing of our house, which had been given to us, showed this plank siding instead of the shingles. The room I had looked into turned out to be the one where I made my office. The windows were made in colonial style with small panes of glass, and they did indeed look like crossbars. The house was new and was empty until we bought it.

Dreams that come true in detail have

been reported many times. Other dreams are equally mysterious. Many people have dreamed of the death of a relative or close friend just at the time of death. Later, by telephone or telegram, they have received word that the person in the dream had died exactly at the time of the dream. There are records of a husband and wife having the same dream the same night. In comparing dreams in the morning they discover this remarkable double dream. There are other cases of people who share a dream sequence. One person dreams the first part, and later the second person dreams the second part. Only when the two parts are put together does the entire dream make sense.

PARAPSYCHOLOGY

Recently a new branch of psychology

has developed. It specializes in studying psychic experiences, including unusual dreams. Those who work in this field are called parapsychologists. Thousands of dreams have been recorded and compared. Controlled experiments have been set up in laboratories.

Some surprising experiments have been carried out at the dream laboratory of Maimonides Medical Center in Brooklyn, New York. There Dr. Montague Ullman, Dr. Stanley Krippner, and others have investigated telepathy during dreams. Telepathy is the silent communication from one mind to another that sometimes happens unexpectedly, even though two people are far apart and are not in touch in any other way. Sigmund Freud suggested that telepathy seemed to work more often during sleep than at other times, and modern research supports this observation.

Here is how the dream experiments were conducted at Maimonides Medical Center. Two volunteers came to spend the night at the dream clinic. These two people did not know each other and did not meet before the experiment. One person went to sleep in a private room. Electrodes had been attached to his head and connected to an EEG machine in another room. There was a public address system between the two rooms. Meanwhile, the other volunteer was taken to a distant room on the same floor. There he was to choose a painting at random from a group of paintings in the room. Then he would try to keep awake through the night and simply look at the painting and think about it. He could write down his impressions of the painting on a pad of paper to help himself concentrate.

Then every time the EEG showed that

Dr. Stanley Krippner monitoring the
EEG at Maimonides Medical Center

the first volunteer was dreaming he was awakened by the loudspeaker in his room and asked to tell the dream, which was tape recorded.

In the morning the content of the dreams was reviewed. This experiment was repeated on different nights with many pairs of volunteers. In almost every case the dreams of the sleeping volunteer contained material found in the painting chosen by the other volunteer! Some volunteers were more successful than others, but in every case at least some telepathy seemed to take place between the pairs of individuals.

In one example reported, a volunteer chose the painting of a famous boxing match between Dempsey and Firpo, by the artist George Bellows. Here is part of a tape recording of one of the dreams of the sleeping volunteer during the night.

George Bellows. *Dempsey and Firpo.* 1924.

There's some kind of a feeling of moving. . . . Ah, something about Mad-

ison Square Garden and a boxing fight.
An angular shape, as if all these things
that I see were in a rectangular frame-
work. There's an angular shape coming
down toward the right, the lower right
as if you were seeing a filming that
took up a whole block. . . . That angular right-hand corner of the picture
is connected with a Madison Square
boxing fight. . . . I had to go to Madison Square Garden to pick up tickets
to a boxing fight. . . .

In most of the experiments the dreamer
did not see the painting as a painting,
but saw objects or people from it as a
part of his own dream story.

How are we to explain all the kinds of
psychic dreams? Parapsychologists are cau-
tious, but their studies suggest that there
is more to reality than the physical world

we have been able to explore. Some mathematicians have suggested that our impression of time is not really accurate. Instead, time is a dimension something like that of length and width. Events seem to happen because we move along the dimension of time. Perhaps what has already happened still exists, and what has not yet happened is already there. Impressions from the subconscious mind seem often to stress the same idea. To the subconscious things may happen all at once, as if there is no time as we experience it when awake.

We know much more about the dream than ever before. We know that we all dream regularly and that our dream work helps us to face problems, to work out solutions, to create new ideas, and to grow as individuals. But the age-old mysteries of the dream are still with us. There are many ideas we are just beginning to study.

Just as the common dream is a natural window to the inner self so it may also be a window to a greater reality than we yet understand.

Recording
Your Own Dreams

With a little patience you can try some interesting experiments with your own dreams. Here are six suggestions that may bring some surprising results.

1. Help yourself to remember more

dreams. You may find that simply being interested and curious will make a
difference. If for any reason a person
becomes interested in his dreams, he is
likely to recall more of them than
usual.

When you first awaken in the morning, lie quietly before jumping out of
bed. Let your mind dwell on the first
thing that pops into it. Try to think
only of this one thing for a while. Do
not let daytime interests interrupt just
yet. If you are lucky, you may find
that this first waking thought actually
has something to do with your last
dream before awakening. It may suddenly remind you of the contents of
the dream. Usually the whole dream
will come to you in a flash. You may
need to try this technique several morn-
ings in a row in order to get results.

2. Keep a notebook of dreams you do remember for a period of a month. Look for important ideas or themes running through them. You may find that a certain topic comes up again and again. Perhaps you have been working on a problem at night without being aware of it. You can discover how your daytime actions have affected your dream themes. You may find that your dreams have suggested actions you were actually able to carry out later.

3. Look for universal symbols in your dream notebook. Do you find kings and queens, small animals, trains, rivers, bridges, roads, or pathways? Do you think the common meanings for them (see pp. 34–37) apply to your dreams?

4. Look for a play on words and numbers in your dreams. Word puns

are common and can often be discov-
ered if you are on the lookout. For instance, in a dream you could be very
bored while staring at a blank black-
board.

One dream researcher tried an experiment to stimulate such dreams. Several volunteers were shown a projection
screen just before going to sleep. Two
pictures were flashed alternately upon
the screen. One was the number 10.
The other was a picture of a hat. Many
of the volunteers reported dreams in
which an officer in uniform—a sailing
captain or an army captain—played a
part. *Captain* was a word combining
cap and *10*!

A mathematician reported dreaming
of numbers that he could not interpret.
One number that appeared in a dream
was 576. He realized that it was the

square of the number 24, that is, 24 x 24 equals 576. But what could it mean? Finally a friend suggested that there were 24 hours in a day. Could the number 24 mean one day? It turned out that the dream made sense when 24 x 24 was interpreted as "day by day." The number 576 stood for this common phrase. And this pun would be logical for a person who knew the shorthand of mathematics.

5. Try giving yourself a nighttime assignment. Before going to sleep, review the work you have done on a problem or a question that has stumped you. Concentrate several evenings, if necessary. If you have given the problem enough attention, you may find that your subconscious will continue to work on it. In the morning, you may remember a dream of a solution or a possible

solution to that particular problem. This method is one way of encouraging creative dream work.

6. Suggest to yourself that you will dream about the future. Think about this idea when you go to bed each night for several nights. Record any dreams you remember no matter how silly they may seem. Enter these in your one-month dream notebook. For a period of four months review your dream notebook at least once every two weeks. You may be surprised at the number of dreams that had some suggestion of future events. In case of a really good prediction, your report written earlier in the notebook stands as proof that you really made such a prediction.

Your experiments may not turn you

into a psychoanalyst, but they will give you some idea of the possibilities to be found in the careful study of dreams. Such research is what will help men to look even deeper into the human personality through the window of the dream.

INDEX

*Indicates illustrations

ABOUT THE AUTHOR

Larry Kettelkamp was born in Harvey, Illinois, and graduated from the University of Illinois, receiving a B.F.A. degree in painting in 1953. The following year he studied illustration at the Pratt Institute, Brooklyn, New York.

After two years' service as a lieutenant in the Army Mr. Kettelkamp returned to Urbana, Illinois, where he joined the staff of Spencer Press. Now he and his family live in New Jersey, and he devotes his time to free-lance writing, illustrating, and designing.

Larry Kettelkamp's first book, *Magic Made Easy*, grew out of a lifelong hobby. He also plays the piano, the classical guitar, and the recorder, and many of his books reflect his strong interest in music. When the author is considering a new book, he often discusses the project with his children and finds their interests are helpful to him in developing his subject.